What the Wind Said!

Matt Simpson
with illustrations by G.W. Jones

GE

GREENWICH EXCHANGE

Greenwich Exchange, London

What the Wind Said!
© Matt Simpson 2008

First published in Great Britain in 2008
All rights reserved

Printed and bound by Q3 Digital/Litho, Loughborough
Tel: 01509 213456

Typesetting, layout and cover design by Jake Campbell, Belfast
Tel: 028 9028 6559

Cover artwork and illustrations by G.W. Jones
© G.W. Jones 2008

Greenwich Exchange Website: www.greenex.co.uk

Cataloguing in Publication Data is available from the British Library

ISBN: 978-1-906075-24-8

for

Emma and Georgia

with love

Contents

Listen   7

Family Matters
In Grandma's Kitchen   10
Granddad's Garden ...   11
Dad's Shed ...   12
Enter the Hero   14
My Phobias   15
When I Grow Up   16
Babies!   17
Well, That's My Excuse   18
Christening   20

School Daze
Miss Mooney   22
Bee Quiet   24
Moonlighting   26
Who Rules School?   27
Spell for the End of Term   28

Would you like to go to Zanzibar?
Magic Carpet   30
Some People Won't Believe Anything You Tell Them   31
Too Many Cooks Save Nine   32
Nodding Off   32
Two Limericks ... and a Quatrain That Never Quite Made It   33
A Scouser's Birthday Card   33
Shedding Light on Things   34
Down with Flu!   36
Think of a Number   37
Big Egg   38
Daft Questions Deserve Daft Answers   39
Call in the Vet   40
A Chewy Toffee Poem   42
Uncle Tobias   44
The Sea Slug and the Shrimp   46

Mad About Footie

Song of a Frustrated Scouse Winger 48

Playing for the School 49

What My Uncle Billy Says 50

Whisked Off 51

No Games Here 52

Animal Crackers

Walking a Friend's Dog – Devon Midnight 54

Cat 55

Reincarnation 56

Cat and Mouse 57

Dog 58

Rhinoceros 59

Silver Back Gorilla 60

Whale Music 61

Fish Eagle 62

Cheetah 64

A Touch of Seasoning

What the Wind Said 66

Nature's Paintbox 67

Come On Spring 68

Spring haiku 69

Summer haiku 70

An Autumn Ghost 71

One Afternoon 72

Summery 73

Cinquain 74

Rooks in Autumn 75

And Finally ... Goodnight

Night Is ... 79

Listen

Sometimes

when
I
lie
in
bed

the
very
best
poems
I
say

I
say
out
loud

inside
my
head.

Family Matters

In Grandma's Kitchen

She lets me chop mint leaves
to make mint sauce;
I do it so fine –
chop, chop, chop
on the old breadboard –
we end up with a sort of
delicious green mud,

and then she lets me peel
and core bramleys for apple pies:
sometimes I trim the pastry
with a bright knife then edge it
all round with a neat fork
so it looks like a small bird's
been walking the rim

and then I stir the custard
yellower and yellower,
and Granddad comes in smiling
from the garden,

it's a nice slow Sunday,
Blackie wags his Sunday-best tail
and we all tuck in.

Granddad's Garden ...

is heady with perfumes,
wallflowers, carnations, velvet roses, lilac:
all the bees and butterflies get tipsy.

He wins prizes. Cups and shields flank
the heavy sideboard clock: Grandma
polishes them with yellow dusters.

I love Granddad showing his garden to me:
sweet peas like bright butterflies,
sky-blue scabious, the fairy hats of columbine.

It's a place that tells you –
just listen to those ring-a-ding Canterbury bells! –
what wonderful things love can do.

Dad's Shed ...

is a shadow-place
of spiders;

dusty, cobwebby,
it smells of rust,

sawdust, glue,
and oily rags;

bits of metal
everywhere,

and things half-fixed
or unmended,

nails in jars,
screws and rock-hard

paint-brushes
a million years old:

the shed's
a secret place

only Dad and the spiders
understand.

Enter the Hero

'Were you born in a field?'
my mother yelled
when I left the door ajar.

'Put the wood in the hole!'
my old man growled
through a mouth like a gangster's scar.

But hadn't they told me I'd been found
under a cabbage or goosegog tree,
all squidgy like a grubby worm
and as tall as a grasshopper's knee?

And because I look a bit of a scruff,
nothing at all like a brand-new pin,
they tell me I am something
the dog has just dragged in!

Some days, some days, some days,
you know you just can't win!

My Phobias

Fear of water
*(When did that face last see a flannel,
those mucky fingers last see soap?)*

Fear of straight lines
*(Why don't you use a ruler?
When did that hair last see a comb?)*

Fear of green things
*(Broccoli's good for you!
Come and help me with these weeds!)*

Fear of neatness
*(Just look at your room! No wonder
You can't find a thing!)*

Fear of animals
*(The dog needs a run!
Your turn to clean the budgie's cage!)*

Fear of being vertical
*(Come on, get up, you lazy-bones!
Are you going to lie on that couch all night?)*

My parents think
I've got all the phobias in the universe.

I let them think I'm *deaf ...*
which, of course, is not the same as being daft!

When I Grow Up

I want to be:

A systems analyst,
A game-show panellist,
A pop star
With a guitar,
A technologist,
A psychologist,
A herpetologist,

A man who studies volcanoes
An ecologist?
No, a seismologist!

I want to be:

Something in the city,
Very pretty,
A fortune teller,
A good speller,

A radar technician,
Always out fishin',
A clever magician,
A cosmetician,
A politician,

A dress designer,
A coal miner,
A good rhymer,
A charmer,
A pig farmer,

A rock and roller,
A South Pole explorer,
A moonwalker,
A New Yorker;

Stinking rich,
A wicked witch,
A private eye,
An engineer,
A life peer,

A DJ
O.K?
A lead singer,
A right winger
For Liverpool,
Cool!

I want to be:

Taller,
Thinner,
A lottery winner!

But if none
Of these can be
I will remain
Yours truly
ME!

Babies!

are self-centred,
        bad-tempered!

I just can't see
        how anything

like THAT,
        was ever, ever ME!

asleep all the time
        or squawking,
no good at talking,
        except
for ga-ga-ga
        and goo-goo-goo ...

what on earth
        good do they do?

Babies smell,
        babies yell!

I said to my mum,
        I told her
babies should be born
        much older!

Well, That's My Excuse

I shouldn't have got up this morning,
I should have stayed in bed,
I've a gloomy sort of feeling,
A heavy weight in my head

Which says today's a no-no,
A black hole of a day,
That tells me I'll sound stupid
Whatever I try to say,

That tells me everybody
Will mess up things I do,
Make my life a misery,
Rotten through and through.

My mates will all ignore me,
Teachers will mark me down,
Mum will nag-nag-nag me
Dad will stare and frown.

I got up this morning
With cotton-wool stuffed in my head.
If I feel like this tomorrow
You bet I stay in bed!

Christening

They wet the baby's head
In church this afternoon.

The baby, wrinkling up its face,
Looked like an angry prune!

Now Dad's just come home from the pub,
It's after half-past ten ...

He went there with Uncle Tom, he said,
To wet it once again!

School Daze

Miss Mooney

Miss Mooney's gone all moony,
not with-it anymore,
staring out the window,
looking at the floor.

Miss Mooney's gone all mopey,
there's this funny look in her eyes,
gazing up at the ceiling,
breathing hefty sighs.

We have a theory:
ever since he came,
that new Mr. Pritchard,
she hasn't been the same!

Mind you, he is dishy
and Year Seven says he's great ...
lucky old Year Seven then,
unlucky us Year Eight!

Miss Mooney's gone all gawpy:
in our Poetry Lesson today
she read *My Love is Like a Red, Red Rose*.
What more is there to say!

Bee Quiet

A bee buzzed into our classroom,
a titchy buzzing machine,
a lumbering, bumbling bumble-bee,
a flying butter bean

with a black-and-yellow jersey on,
madly flapping the air
with a pair of much too diddy wings.
'Nobody move!' said Sir.

We were stiller than ever we'd been before,
stiller than statues we were.
'If no silly person annoys it
it'll fly away,' said Sir.

It blundered into the gerbils' cage,
then over the tank it hovered
where Fred, our placid goldfish, swims
who didn't seem much bothered.

At last it found the window
and into the sunlight it flew,
chuffed to be out in the open
where the honeysuckle grew.

'Now I know what I should do
when you lot make a din:
bring me in a bumble-bee!'
said Sir with a sarky grin.

This afternoon was something else;
in the middle of doing Spelling
a wasp flew into the classroom,
soon everyone was yelling

and dodging about and ducking it.
Before the beast had gone
there was panic, there was mutiny,
it dive-bombed everyone.

And there was Sir shouting
'Nobody move! Stay cool!'
The wasp flew at him like a dart
and buzzed him out of school.

Moonlighting

Our teacher bicycles home each day
and – do you know what? –
he hangs upside down in the wardrobe
next to his striped shirts
and the grotty ties he always wears,

and whenever there's a full moon
he comes flapping out like an old
black umbrella, flap-flapping
and squeak-squeaking ... on the look-out

for jugulars! He has teeth like
an alligator ... and when he finds
a juicy neck you can hear him slurp-slurp
just like my old granddad with tomato soup!

Who Rules School?

I, said the Head, like a fussy old hen,

I, said the Teacher, with my red pen,

I, said the Caretaker, because I have the keys,

I, said the Cleaner, the whole world agrees,

I, said the Dinner-lady, sloshing out mince,

I, said the Governor, with pounds and pence,

Us, say the Government, with our curricula,

I, said the Nurse, with hands that tickle yer,

I, said the Computer, with all my data,

I, said Detention, I can keep you in later,

I, said the Radiator, I can freeze you or fry you.

Us, said exams, we test you and try you,

Who rules school? The wind, the rain,

and term-time coming round again.

Spell for the End of Term

Who is it says that spells don't work?
      Whoever they are Look Out!
I made one up last Saturday
      That should leave no kind of doubt.

I said the alphabet backwards,
      Concocted a magic brew
From things I dare not mention.
      Don't you wish you knew!

Well sort of things like bat-spit
      And some hairs from a pharaoh's chin,
Some bits of twine, some old red wine
      And one white shark's black fin.

When Mam and Dad went to Tesco's
      To get the shopping done
I went up in the attic
      To start my bit of fun.

So look out, Mrs Faraday
      Who screams at us in class
At ten-past two next Friday
      You will turn into an Ass!

With long grey ears all hairy
      And a screechy loud hee-haw!
This is - before we all break up -
      My present to Class Four.

Would you like to go to Zanzibar ?

Magic Carpet

Would you like to go to Zanzibar?
Would you like to visit Tashkent?
Eat Turkish Delight in Trebizond
Or chocolates in old Ghent?

Would you like to slip off to Cyprus
Or slide away to Greece?
Maybe zoom over the Andes,
Spend a week in Nice?

Do you like the sound of Sligo?
Do you fancy a month in Brazil?
Climb up on my Magic Carpet,
The whole thing's going to be brill!

Some People Just Won't Believe Anything You Tell Them

I once went up to a tiger and said 'How are you, son?'

He opened his jaws to answer. You should have seen me run!

I hacked my way through the jungle, wind-surfed the Irish Sea.

When I got home my mother said 'You're too late for your tea!'

'But, Mum, there was THIS TIGER ...' 'Oh was there, my dear son?

Of course there was, my darling! Now pull the other one!'

Too Many Cooks Save Nine

It made my hair chatter,
My teeth all stood on end,
It was certain I was going
Straight around the bend!

It made my ears pop out on stalks,
It made my eyes burn red,
Someone was walking on my grave
And I wasn't even dead!

I went weak at the armpits,
My knees began to bleep,
Till suddenly next Friday
I woke up fast asleep!

Nodding Off

Head down on the pillow,
Drifting deep-down deep,
I had the deepest dream of all:
I dreamt I was asleep!

Nothing upset me in my dream,
There was no kind of horror.
I simply woke next morning,
And found it was tomorrow!

Two Limericks ...
and a Quatrain That Never Quite Made It

The trouble with my friend Germaine
Is she just won't go out in the rain.
When the rain starts to pelt
She thinks she will melt
And go gurgling away down the drain.

Said Mr Charles Darwin, 'By golly!
Man's next to the angels? What folly!
There's a far better jape!
He descends from an ape,
Once lived up a tree! Ain't that jolly?'

A Scouser's Birthday Card

Toodaze yor sumfink berfdee, Ma,
I want yer terrav a gud time,
So t cheer yerrup on y berfdee, Mam,
I've rittf-yer diss pome!

Shedding Light on Things

I was watching this funny green fellow,
he had just one eye, like a pear,
standing at a corner of the street
busily flip-flopping his green webbed feet
and flailing green arms in the air.

And because I've got this Translating Machine
I can pass on what he said,
though to you it would sound like giggles
and on paper would look like squiggles
or numbers bounced about on their head.

He was talking to a lamppost
that rose above him straight,
his little green body was swaying
and what I heard him saying
was *Which planet are you from, mate?*

35

Down with Flu!

I've a bag code,
fluey and flemmy
in me node;

feel like somebobby's
stuffed
a hod wet towel
insibe
me achin' heb;

I've a scratchy frob
in me throbe,
me chest's full
ob frobspawn;

I wheeze and explose
into me hankersneeze,
I tishoo-tishoo-tishoo
into me tishoo;

I've a bag code
in me node,
and I'm feb up,
really feb up,

really, really, really
feb up here in beb.

Think of a Number

0 is really a joined-up **C**,

1 plus **3** equals **B**,

2 is a swan on a flowing stream,

4 is, look, a windsurfer's dream!

5 and **6** are some inside bits from a broken clock,

7 is an axe for chopping a block,

8 is a twisted party balloon,

9's going to fall over pretty soon,
watch him at his clever tricks
roll right round and be a **6**!

Big Egg

Who never needed egging on at school?

Who was a tough egg always playing it cool?

Who, shelling out, was never mean?

Who was bald as a coot, hard-boiled as a bean?

Who won the egg-and-spoon race every year?

Who was forever in hot water but never showed fear?

Who never studied Wallcraft and How not to Fall?

Who was always sunnyside up, brightest of all?

Who thought he had it cracked? Who badly gambled?

Who ended up horribly scrambled?

Raise your glasses in a buttered toast

To poor old Humpty Dumpty's ghost!

Fate can be a rotten egg, fate can be so grim.

Poor old Humpty Dumpty. The yoke is now on him!

Daft Questions Deserve Daft Answers

How long do you think this is?
(Half as twice as much!)

Who do you think you are talking to?
(The Archbishop of Canterbury!)

What time do you call this?
(I call it Fred!)

Am I talking to myself?
(Pardon?)

Were you born in a field?
(Moo!)

What do you think your dad will say?
(Moo!)

Are you even listening to me?
(Who?)

Whose leg do you think you're pulling, eh?
(The Archbishop of Canterbury's!)

Is there anything between your ears?
(Space, the Final Frontier!)

Are you daft or what?
(Or what!)

WHAT DID YOU SAY JUST THEN?
(Nothing, Mum, honest!)

Call in the Vet

Sir Silas Debret
Had to call in the vet
When the pigs in his sty
Turned blue.

'Dear Doctor,' he sighed,
'I'm quite mortified.
Pray tell me, sir, what
I should do.'

The vet took some soap,
A large stethoscope
And went in the sty
For a look.

Yes, the pigs were quite blue
And just what to do
Didn't appear
In his book.

He thought and he wondered,
He mused and he pondered
Until he came up with
The answer.

'If I may be so bold
These pigs are too cold!
What they need is some
Warm woolly pants, sir!'

Sir Silas Debret
To no-one's regret
Set all his farm-hands
A-knitting,

Till after two Sundays
The pigs' thermal undies
Were finally ready
For fitting.

Even though it was snowing,
Soon the pigs were all glowing,
Snowflakes just
melted away.

They all looked so pink
You couldn't help think
Of cherry trees
Blossoming in May.

'By George, Doctor Figgs,
I've not seen my pigs
Ever before
Look so frisky,'

Beamed Sir Silas Debret
Shaking hands with the vet
And pouring him out
Some malt whisky.

A Chewy Toffee Poem

UH GLUG GLEWING GLOGGEE
UH GLEAT IG GALL GUH GLIME

GUNGDAY
GLUESDAY
GENSDAY
GLURSDAY
GLIDAY
GLATTERDAY
GLUNDAY

GLEWING GLOGGEE'S GLUGGLY

GLORNING
GLOON
ANG GLIGHT

EGGLEGGLY GLEAGLE GLOGGEE
GLAT GLAKES GLOR GLEEG GALL GLACK

Uncle Tobias

My uncle, Tobias Sebastian Prune
Was the very first man from Wigan
To walk upon the moon.

He yanked his lunar barge-boots on,
Adjusted his life-support:
'One giant step for Wigan'
Was his one abiding thought.

He went there to gather data
From a great big dusty crater,
Collected funny globules
And loads of tiny nodules
Which he fed into a shredder
To test the moon for Cheddar.

He hopped, he bounced, he floated
Like a great gas-filled balloon
Among the unatmospheric mountains
Of the grey, dust-covered moon.

In his tightly pumped-up space-suit:
He looked masterful and cute,
Lights bleeped and blipped
As he weightlessly skipped
Back to his loony spacecraft
With all his lunar loot.

When he landed back in Wigan,
'What was it like?' they said.
'It's made of black pudding,' he told them
and trundled off to bed.

45

The Sea Slug and the Shrimp

A sea slug wooed a shy pink shrimp
The best part of a year,
Till the sea slug said one Wednesday
Let's get hitched, my dear.

Miss Shrimp went two shades pinker,
Oh, Samuel! she stuttered,
*I think that is the sweetest thing
That you have ever uttered.*

In the wreck of a Spanish galleon,
Among its sparkling treasure,
They found a golden wedding ring
Perfectly made to measure.

Sid Dolphin was the Best Man,
The bridesmaids the Jellyfish Girls,
Jim Lobster gave the bride away
In her gown of seaweed and pearls.

A Bishop conducted the Service,
The Most Reverend Eli Clam,
Who married Sam to his Amy
In the waters off Japan.

They went to live near Australia
In a tide that's warm and slow
And swam forever happily
Where the coloured corals grow.

Mad About Footie!

Song of a Frustrated Scouse Winger

Over 'ere with it, Charlie!
Duz it 'ave to take all year!
On me 'ed, son, on me 'ed then,
let's 'ave it over 'ere!

Their back line is 'opeless,
their goalie's a gormless clot,
now knock it over quick terruz,
I'll put it in the pot!

Cum 'ed, Charlie, pass it, lad!
Are y'gunna take all year?
To me left foot, me left foot, Charlie!
Curl it over 'ere!

D'y'raffter hog it to y'self,
fumble it down the right
while I am waitin' on the left
a gapin' goal in sight?

An open goal just dead ahead
and 'ere is me ONSIDE
with you greedy-guts 'angin' on to the ball
and bangin' it yards wide!

Playing for the School

Looking lively, running out,
yellow strip, boots all shiny with dew.

November morning. Air brisk on cheeks,
on knees. Puffing clouds. Then Sir

shrilling his whistle and black rooks
coughing in the sticks of trees.

Booted ball thudding, slithering
like a greased pig. Ninety minutes'

muscled battling. Mud all over.

Bruised warriors trudging in.
Tired. Winners. Hot as boiled eggs.

What My Uncle Billy Says

Footballers! They get away with murder,
earn more than is good for them,
swank about the place in flash cars,
Porsches, Beamers; get drunk,
pick fights in big posh discos,
some blonde bimbo always in tow;

cynically go where the money is,
Italy, Japan - or on telly advertising
stupid things like shower gel,
potato crisps. And on the field,
spitting, swearing and pulling at
other players' shirts to get the ball;

and then, when they score, hugging
and kissing, rolling round like acrobats.
He'd pay them what factory workers get,
no more no less!

And all because I said I wanted to play
For Liverpool ... and he's an Evertonian!

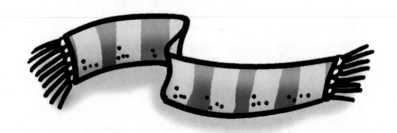

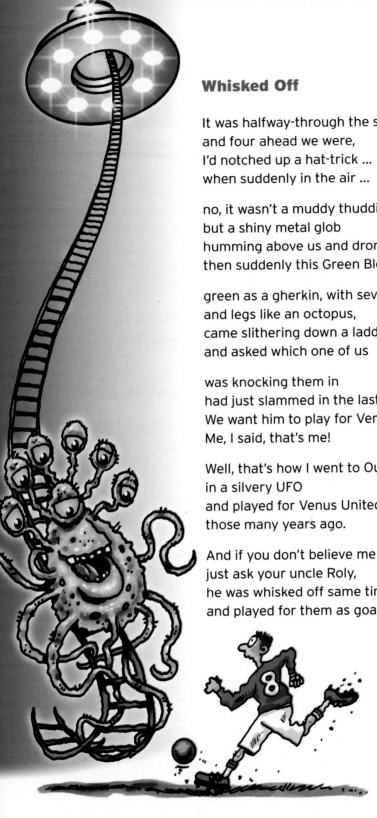

Whisked Off

It was halfway-through the second half
and four ahead we were,
I'd notched up a hat-trick ...
when suddenly in the air ...

no, it wasn't a muddy thudding ball
but a shiny metal glob
humming above us and droning ...
then suddenly this Green Blob ...

green as a gherkin, with seven great eyes
and legs like an octopus,
came slithering down a ladder
and asked which one of us

was knocking them in
had just slammed in the last three.
We want him to play for Venus, he said ...
Me, I said, that's me!

Well, that's how I went to Outer Space
in a silvery UFO
and played for Venus United
those many years ago.

And if you don't believe me
just ask your uncle Roly,
he was whisked off same time as me
and played for them as goalie!

51

No Games Here

Don't kick the ball
Against that wall!
That's the house
          of Mr Grundy!

He don't like noise
Or little boys
Especially
          on Sunday!

Animal Crackers

Walking a Friend's Dog – Devon Midnight

I just can't see,
don't know
where anything is.

I have to imagine hedges,
the sky, the lane ahead.
Tonight is as black
as loudspeakers,
as peppercorns, as rain-
soaked soil, as black as
a mole's eyesight
underground.

It doesn't bother the dog.
He can see with his wet
black nose, snuffling
at hedges. He can tell where
a fox has shouldered through,
can hear field-mice scratch.

Tonight is black
as lofts, as cupboards
under stairs, so dark
I'm scared ...

me ... a grown man
from the phosphorescent city ...
asking Is it time to turn back home?
Are you still there?

Cat

Cat's sneaky,
leaps on my lap
with sudden claws
like nettle stings.

And now she is
tucking herself away –
O so tidily – right down
to her Chinese eyes.

Purrs like a lawn-mower ...

Yes, but her ears, her ears
are watching something
that hops and twitters
worm-hungry
among the wet petunias.

Reincarnation

I'm
putting my name down
to come back as
a cat,
like our Cleo.

I'll snooze
the whole of my next life away,
letting my pride and joy,
my tail,
find only the warmest
places:

that corner of the garden
the sun lingers
round the roots of the laburnum,

that spot on the landing
where the hot water pipes run
under the floorboards.

Whenever I want to
I'll stretch myself
arching my back ecstatically

and dig my claws into
the bedside rug,
a plump cushion,
someone's lap.

I'll go mooching and mousing
by the light of the moon
and come home any old time I like!

You can guarantee
someone will always
be there

to feed me, stroke me,
make me purr.

Cat and Mouse

Skitterings in the shrubbery.
Trembling, twitching leaves.

Cat in shadow. Cat on the lawn.
Still as brick. Intent as the moon.

A pounce, a crash!

Enter Cat with mouse moustache!

Dog

I'm a lollopy dog,
A lumbering slouch of a dog,
A flop-down-in-a-corner dog,

Not like the dog next-door,
That yapping gerbil of a thing,
That maniac wasp of a pooch.

I'm a reluctant dog,
A don't-bother-me-now dog,
A do-I-really-have-to dog.

Not like next door's crazy yapper,
That nip-your-ankles
Pesky miniature chainsaw thing.

I'm a comfortable dog,
A flop-down-with-a-great-big-sigh dog,
One of those I'll-love-you-if-you-love-me dogs,

A slobbery, big-eyed daft-dog dog.

Rhinoceros

God simply got bored and started doodling
with ideas he'd given up on, scooping off the floor
bits and bobs and sticking them together:
the tail of a ten-ton pig he'd meant for Norway,

the long skull of a too-heavy dinosaur,
the armour plating of his first version of
the hippo, an unpainted beak of a toucan

stuck on back to front, a dash of tantrums
he intended for the Abyssinian owl, the same
awful grey colour he'd used for landscaping the moon.

And tempted to try it with the batteries,
he set it down on the wild plains of Africa,
grinned at what he saw and let it run.

Silver Back Gorilla

Through undergrowth and the gauze nets of mosquitoes,
solid as an all-in wrestler, a gorilla takes
his morning's slowly-waddled muscular stroll,
shaking leaves on the lower slopes of his extinct
volcano. The earth smells rich and mossy-damp
in his rain forest; vines and herbs scent his trail,
his track, eating another day away – juicy leaves,
the soggy pith of his banana trees, the sweet
stringiness of his bamboo. See him shin up trunks,
slide down like a weightless astronaut;
hear him bark and beat his bongo chest saying
Keep off my grass! Keep out of my paradise! This is
my heaven, my peace and plenty! Go away!

Whale Music

Great underwater zeppelin,
sea-salt singer,
hoovering up
the soupy oceans,
the minestrone waves!

When I first heard
your thar-she-blows,
your old grampus
huffing and puffing,

I thought you were
some enormous sea-horse
snorting ...

and when I saw
your tail-flukes flop
and plunge

I thought you were
a huge black angel
falling into the ocean ...

O submarine gargler,
I have listened
to your sad, mysterious songs,
your clickings
and crooning
fathoms down

and wished
there was a way
of singing songs
to you.

Fish Eagle

Eyes lasering
through acres of sky,
into wind-ruffled water,
intent on the waving
shadows of fish,
on the faintest v of fins
breaking the surface ...

then falling in a blur
through wild space,
stabbing the lake
with the deadly hooks
of his talons,

whizzing up
skywards again,
with the waggling
last bit of life
of a two-pound trout.

Cheetah

Eyes glaring in dead earnest, full of fire,
she means business, has cubs to feed;
stalking's her business, she knows it inside out,
ask the gazelle or wildebeest.

She has stationed her forepaws on the grey trunk
of a fallen tree, is listening for the slightest shiver
in the grass, nostrils tensed for the merest sniff
of hot-blooded food ... or danger.

She takes her time, judges her moment,
and then, whoosh, she's away like a souped-up sports car,
pistons pounding, oiled to perfection, until,
head-high, she lugs their meal back home.

A Touch of Seasoning

What the Wind Said

Where to, Wind? Where to?
Round the chimneys, down the flue.

After that? What after that?
Going to spin off someone's hat.

Where will that be? Tell us where.
In the centre of town square.

Whose hat is it? Tell us who.
Mrs Hoity-Toity Fortescue.

Where to then? Where to then?
Chasing mist across the fen.

Which way, Wind? Now which way?
Over the fields and miles away.

Nature's Paintbox

In Spring the sky is blue and bright,
Autumn's blue is bold,
Summer's blue's a cheerful blue,
Winter's is ice-cold.

White in Spring is brand-new lambs,
In Autumn white turns grey,
Summer's white's an ice-cream-white,
Winter's is snow all day.

Spring's red is tulips,
Autumn's a fading rose,
Summer's red is sunburnt skin,
Winter's a sniffly red-raw nose.

Spring's favourite colour is green,
Autumn's favourite's brown,
Summer warms the colours up,
Winter cools them down.

Come On Spring

When will it be Spring?
When will it be Spring?
I'm tired of snow
And ice and sleet,
Winds that knock you
Off your feet
And blow you about like anything.
Oh, when will it be Spring?

Whenever will Spring come?
Whenever will Spring come?
Slush all gone
Down gurgling grids,
Warmth in the sun
And all the kids
No longer numb.
Oh, whenever will Spring come?

Come, fill our gardens with daffodils,
Gorgeous golden daffodils!
Let's see green shoots
And tiny tadpoles wiggling about
In their birthday suits.
Let the buds all sprout!
Let's hear your fanfares, daffodils!

Spring haiku

Such green porpoise snouts
nosing up through the black soil ...
here come hyacinths!

Splodges of bright paint ...
It's time to redecorate!
say the primulas.

Listen! tuning up!
The daffodils are testing
out their trumpets.

Thrushes in the old
beech hedge already stashing
Easter eggs away.

Summer haiku

Deep in white blossoms,
perky about his prospects,
the year's first bee!

Rain shower over ...
such velvety-plush odours.
Must be wallflowers!

Flitting, fluttering,
weaving wild nothings, a pair
of white butterflies!

Only just see him!
Titchy black dot. A skylark!
Listen, just listen!

An Autumn Ghost

I am the ghost of the broomstick
Old Jinny Green Teeth rode.

On autumn days you find me
Sweeping leaves down the road.

It's what always happens to broomsticks
When their witches are dead,

They become the winds of autumn
Whistling round your head.

One Afternoon

The pitter-patter rain suddenly ceased.
Sky held its breath. Then a cloud parted

and a bright beam of warm sunlight
shot right down into the garden.

Everything started smiling. Birds struck up
a silvery chorus. And, oh, that sudden

knock-out scent of velvet wallflowers
and roses with little twinkly beads of rain

like diamonds in among the petals.
Roof tiles steamed and windows gleamed.

I remember saying Let's open the door
and ask Summer in to tea.

Summery

I love those pure-white summer clouds
That drift across blue skies,
The knock-out scent of meadowsweet,
Willows full of sighs
When a breeze goes tickling their branches,
And a lark decides to rise.

I love lying in long grasses
That insects scuffle among,
Where bees helicopter over flowers,
And a stream glug-glugs along,
The lark above right out of sight
But cramming the sky with song.

This is the time for picnics,
Cherry-cake and tea
Poured hot from stubby vacuum flasks,
Plates balanced on your knee,
With cheese and brown-sauce sandwiches,
In the shade of a sycamore tree.

Cinquain

Fumbling
little hummer,
a bumblebee bumbling,
there in the foxgloves rumbling:
Summer!

Rooks in Autumn

It's here again! A sudden chill in the air,
a bright sharpness in the look of things,
the sun squeezed like a lemon.

The rooks know too. They are building
raucously in the high trees. The trees themselves
have felt a chilly touch shudder through them

as if something sinister's sliding up the branches,
an invisible ice-cold snaky thing. Leaves now
giving up the ghost, becoming ghosts.

Nearly time for the wind to sweep them up,
swirl them along the avenue. And we know
it's time for scarves, gloves and cough sweets,

hot Bovril and crumpets dripping honey,
for pullovers to come yawning out of drawers, and time
for draught-excluders to get down to serious work again.

And Finally ... Goodnight

Night is ...

headlights switching on in cars
in the coming dark,
children shouted in from play
emptying the park,

lights flicked on in bedrooms,
street lamps suddenly humming,
curtains getting swished across,
the Sandman coming,

putting fresh pyjamas on,
tucking in the sheet,
stories from a story book,
hot-water-bottle feet,

head upon the pillow
trying to settle down ...
what's that moving on the door?
... just a dressing gown!

rubbing itchy eyeballs,
hugging Teddy Bear,
want a drink of water!
Mummy someone's there!

turning over on your side,
pretending not to peep,
gone before you know it
deep-down into ...

Acknowledgements

Some of the poems in this selection or versions of them appeared in *The Pigs' Thermal Underwear* by Matt Simpson, Headland Publications, 1994, and in *Sandwich Poets/Lost Property Box*, Macmillan 1995/1998.

And some appeared in the following anthologies: *A Sea Creature Ate My Teacher*, Macmillan, 2000; *Bonkers for Conkers*, Macmillan, 2003; *Chasing the Sun*, Simon & Schuster, 1991; *Cheating at Conkers*, Longman, 1994; *'Ere We Go*, Macmillan, 1993; *Football Fever*, Oxford, 2000; *Frogs in Clogs*, Macmillan, 2005; *Heinemann English Programme 1*, 1995; *Hubble Bubble*, Hodder, 2003; *I Love You Football*, Hodder, 2003; *I'm Telling on You*, Macmillan, 1999; *I Remember, I Remember*, Macmillan, 2003; *It's Raining Cats and Dogs*, Blackie, 1994; *Key Stage 3 Targeting Level 4 in Year 7*, DIES, 2003; *Lifelines*, WWF, 2002; *Parent Free Zone*, Macmillan, 1997; *Poems about Seasons*, Hodder, 2000; *Poems for 8 Year Olds*, Macmillan, 1999; *Poems for Year 4*, Macmillan, 2002; *Poems to Make Your Friends Laugh*, Oxford, 2003; *Poems to Annoy Your Parents*, Oxford, 2003; *Read Me*, Macmillan, 1998; *Seasonal Poetry: Autumn*, Wayland, 1990; *Sunlight Starbright*, Julia MacRea, 1995; *The Word Party*, Macmillan, 1991; *Read Me 2*, Macmillan, 1998; *You Just Can't Win*, Blackie, 1991; *The Poetry Book*, Dolphin, 1996; *The Poetry Store*, Hodder, 2005; *The Rhyme Riot*, Macmillan, 2002; *The Second Poetry Kit*, A & C Black, 1990; *The Secret Life of Teachers*, Macmillan, 1996/2005; *The Usborne Book of Children's Poems*, 1990; *The Works Poems for Key Stage 2*, Macmillan, 2006; *The Works 4*, Macmillan, 2005; *The Works 5*, Macmillan, 2006; *This Way Up – Texts 3*, Otava (Finland), 2001; *The Young Oxford Book of Football Stories*, 1998; *We Was Robbed*, Macmillan, 1997; *Who Rules School?*, Macmillan, 1998; *Unzip Your Lips*, Macmillan, 1998; *Unzip Your Lips Again*, Macmillan, 1999; *Wild and Wonderful*, WWF, 2002; *Word Play – Animals and Night*, BBC, 1990.

Some poems were broadcast on BBC Radio 4 and 'Granddad's Garden' was part of a television programme (CBBC/CBEEBIES) on National Poetry Day 2005.